How to Save Tax Dollars When You Sell Your House

OFFERED BY

YOUR REAL ESTATE PROFESSIONAL

RICHARD ROBINSON, C.P.A.

International Standard Book Number *0-88462-370-X*

Copyright © 1978

by Development Systems Corporation

Published by Real Estate Education Company/Chicago

10   9   8   7   6   5   4   3   2

This publication is designed to provide accurate and authoritative information in
regard to the subject matter covered. It is sold with the understanding that the
publisher is not engaged in rendering legal, accounting, or other professional
service. If legal advice or other expert assistance is required, the services of a
competent professional person should be sought.—*From a Declaration of Principles
jointly adopted by a Committee of the American Bar Association and a Committee of Publishers.*

Dedicated to the
greatest little tax shelter
in the world—your
house and mine!

INTRODUCTION

The aim of this book is to tell you about the many wonderful tax benefits of the personal residence so that you can save tax dollars if and when you ever sell your house. It will teach you all about these tax benefits and how they work. And this book gives you handy worksheet forms that will help you to keep a record of the information you need in order to take advantage of these benefits and save some of those precious and expensive tax dollars.

Tax knowledge can save you a lot of money—your money! That's why it is so important that you know what's happening tax-wise as well as real estate-wise when you sell your house.

WELCOME TO THE WONDERFUL WORLD OF TAX SHELTERS

Your personal residence is one of the finest tax-sheltered investments in America today.

Even though it is a "personal" and not a "business" asset, it provides you with current deductions for interest and real estate taxes *and* qualifies for capital gain treatment if sold at a profit. And you can exclude or postpone all or some of this gain if you qualify for certain tax benefits available to you when you sell your house.

High inflation rates and demand for housing have caused the market value of your house to go up—up—up! And if you don't understand how the tax laws work before you sell your house, you might get stuck with a big income tax on this gain.

But fortunately, there are many wonderful tax benefits available to you when you own and sell your own personal residence. Let's preview some of them right now:

- First you will learn how to compute the gain when you sell your house. This sounds like I am starting at the wrong end, but I'm really not. You see, the gain you make on the sale might be taxable— so, before you can appreciate how to reduce or postpone the gain tax-wise, you have to know how much the gain is and how to figure it.

- Then you will discover how to postpone all or part of the gain on your old house when you go out and buy another house. There are just two simple rules to follow to get this tax-free exchange benefit. I explain them to you in this book.

- Next you will learn about improvements and how to keep score, so that you can deduct the cost of these improvements when you sell

7

your house. And you will learn how improvements on your new house can sometimes reduce the taxable gain when you sell your old house.

- Over 55 years of age? If so, you might want to exclude all or some of the gain when you sell your old house. This book will teach you how this works—you might even qualify right now!

- Sometimes these great tax benefits can work together. If you are over 55, and sell your old house at a gain, you might postpone only part of your gain if you buy another house. Then you can elect to exclude the balance of the gain under the "over 55" exclusion benefit.

- Did you sell your old house before July 27, 1978, and pay a lot of income taxes because you decided not to buy a new house? If so, this book will show you how to "reach back" and bring that gain forward so that you can exclude it under the "over 55" exclusion.

- Many people sell their house because they are changing jobs and moving to a new location. This book will teach you how the moving expense deduction works and how you might qualify to deduct some of the costs of selling your house right off the top of your income.

- You will also learn about other tax benefits for homeowners in the Revenue Act of 1978. These include changes in the capital gains tax rate and information on how you might qualify to "rollover" 2 houses in the same 18-month period and qualify both sales as tax-free exchanges.

Well, enough of what we are going to do. Let's get started now and do it!

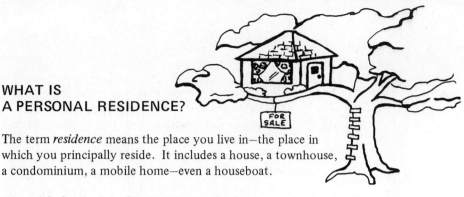

WHAT IS
A PERSONAL RESIDENCE?

The term *residence* means the place you live in—the place in which you principally reside. It includes a house, a townhouse, a condominium, a mobile home—even a houseboat.

To qualify for the benefits described in this book, you must own your personal residence. Even if you still owe the mortgage company a bundle on the property, it's all your personal residence for income tax purposes. And it can be located in any country in the world.

SOME TERMS WE WILL BE USING

It sure helps to know what some of the terms mean—exactly—when you are trying to learn something new. You know how involved and complicated our tax laws are. Here are some terms that I will be using and a brief explanation of what they mean to us. (I will introduce more along the way as we need them.)

OLD HOUSE:	the principal personal residence you now own and live in or are selling. If you own more than one property at the same time, only one can be your "personal residence."
NEW HOUSE:	the personal residence you are going to buy and live in—your replacement residence if you are selling your **old house.** Even though I use the term **new house,** I mean new *only to you.* It does not have to be brand new; it might even be physically older than your **old house.**
ADJUSTED BASIS:	the tax cost that you can deduct when you sell your **old house.** Generally, the **adjusted basis** is the total of the original cost of the **old house** plus the cost of improvements you have added during the time you owned it.

9

SELLING EXPENSES:	all expenses of the sale when you sell your ***old house.*** Examples are: sales commissions paid, escrow fees, title policy fees, recording fees, etc. It does not include interest or taxes; these are itemized deductions. (If you get stuck with a prepayment penalty when you pay off your old mortgage, it's interest, and you can deduct it in full as an itemized deduction the year you pay it.) Loan payoffs and impound account adjustments are personal, and are not counted as ***selling expenses.***

HOW TO COMPUTE THE GAIN
WHEN YOU SELL YOUR OLD HOUSE

When you sell your ***old house,*** the gain is the difference between your total cost in the house (the ***adjusted basis***) and what you receive from the sale after paying all the ***selling expenses.*** (This is called the ***amount realized.***) Or, putting it in more technical terms, the gain on the sale of your ***old house*** is the excess of the ***amount realized*** on the sale over the ***adjusted basis*** of the ***old house.***

EXAMPLE:

Sales price of old house		$90,000
Deduct selling expenses		6,000
Amount realized		$84,000
Original cost	50,000	
Add improvements	6,000	
Adjusted basis	$56,000	
Deduct adjusted basis		56,000
Gain on sale		$28,000

10

Here is a new term:

> *AMOUNT REALIZED:* the sales price of the **old house** less the **selling expenses**. The **amount realized** is usually not all cash; it includes the payoff of your mortgage loans.

A CLOSER LOOK AT THE AMOUNT REALIZED

Many people don't understand what the **amount realized** really is; they think it's always the amount of cash you get out of the sale. *Don't you believe it!*

Most of the time, people owe a mortgage on the **old house** and it is paid off out of the sale. But this does not reduce the **amount realized**. The net cash (after payoff) that the seller receives is just that—the net cash. Again, the **amount realized** is usually not all cash; it includes the payoff of your mortgage loans.

SOME IMPORTANT POINTS YOU NEED TO KNOW

These points are very important:

1. The gain on the sale of your **old house** can result in taxable income unless you qualify to use one or more of the tax-saving benefits.

2. If you suffer a loss on the sale of your **old house,** it's a personal loss and is *not* deductible.

3. If called upon by the Internal Revenue Service (IRS), you will have to prove all the figures used to compute the gain (or loss). If you can't prove some of these, you might receive a big fat tax bill in the mail.

4. Notice in our example that the cost of the improvements was *added to the original cost* of the **old house.** This increased the **adjusted basis** deduction.

11

5. Mortgage loan payoffs when you sell your *old house* are not deductible, and do not reduce the *amount realized.*

A SUPER TAX BENEFIT—THE TAX-FREE EXCHANGE

Many people believe that the tax-free exchange applies only to business property. Not so!

There is a special provision in the Internal Revenue Code (Section 1034) for people who sell their *old house* at a gain and want to qualify for a tax-free exchange. That means no taxable income on the gain, and therefore, many tax dollars saved.

If you qualify for this benefit, it is mandatory to postpone the gain; you can't pay tax on it even if you want to! And, if you qualify, this provision can be used in combination with your election to exclude the first $100,000 of gain when you sell your *old house.* More on this later.

Let's say that you have sold, or are planning to sell, your *old house* at a gain. You can qualify for a tax-free exchange, and therefore not have to pay income tax on the gain, if you meet these requirements:

1. You must buy and occupy a *new house* (replacement residence) sometime during the 3-year period starting 18 months *before* you sell the *old house* and ending 18 months *after* you sell the *old house.* In almost all cases, the date of sale is the date on which the sale closes and title passes to the buyer.

   and

2. The replacement cost of your *new house* must be equal to or more than the adjusted sales price of your *old house. Adjusted sales price* is a new term, but don't worry, we will learn exactly what it means a little later.

12

A LOOK AT THE REPLACEMENT TIME PERIOD

The *replacement time period* extends from the 18 months *before* through the 18 months *after* the day on which you sell your *old house.* It looks like this:

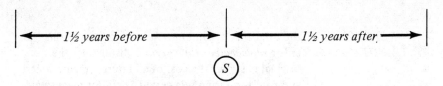

$\left(\,S\,\right)$ is the date on which you sell your *old house.*

It is not necessary to buy and occupy your *new house* on the same date. You will qualify if you buy the *new house* sometime during the 3-year period *and* occupy it as your personal residence sometime during this same period. The 2 dates do not have to be the same. Here is an example to illustrate this:

> *You sell your old house on February 10, 1980. Prior to that, on November 15, 1979, you had found your new house and purchased it. After your old house was sold, you moved into your new house, on February 19, 1980.*

> *Both dates fall within the 3-year time period. You qualify!*

If you build your own *new house* (or have it built for you) on your own lot, there's a special 6-month extension of the 18 months *after* you sell your *old house.* This gives you more time to complete the construction and move in. But make sure that the construction is started sometime during the regular 3-year *replacement time period* or you won't qualify!

There are some special rules that suspend the *replacement time period* for men and women serving on extended active duty in the armed forces after they sell their *old house.* These rules are somewhat complicated; if you need more information you should contact your own taxperson or the IRS.

NOW A LOOK AT THE REPLACEMENT COST REQUIREMENT

REPLACE-
MENT COST: the total cost of your **new house** incurred during the entire **replacement time period.** It includes the original cost *plus* the cost of all improvements added and paid for during this period. *Paid for* means paid by cash (or check) or the giving of a note payable. Financing the construction of a new swimming pool, for example, would count as an improvement for the entire cost of the pool.

VERY IMPORTANT POINT: you don't have to reinvest all the cash proceeds from the sale of your *old house* in your *new house.* You can cash out on your *old house* and pay little or nothing down on your *new house* (if you can find such a deal) and still qualify for the tax-free exchange. The amount of cash money reinvested is immaterial, because both cash and notes (the new mortgage) count as *replacement cost.*

REVIEW

Let's take a look and see where we are so far:

- If you sell your *old house* at a gain, the gain is a capital gain and is realized for tax purposes.

- The gain on the sale of your *old house* is the difference between the *amount realized* and the *adjusted basis.* It has nothing to do with the mortgages or how much cash you receive from the sale.

14

- You won't have to recognize the gain for income taxes (and pay tax on it) if you qualify for a tax-free exchange on the sale. In fact, under this provision, you can't pay the tax even if you want to.

- You qualify for this super tax benefit by purchasing and occupying a **new house** sometime during the 3-year **replacement time period** and your **replacement cost** is equal to or more than the **adjusted sales price** of the **old house.**

- Remember, if you construct your **new house** or go on active duty in the armed forces, there are different rules about the **replacement time period.**

THE MAGIC NUMBER—THE ADJUSTED SALES PRICE

This is the magic number. The **adjusted sales price** is the amount that you must reinvest in your **new house** in order to qualify for the full tax-free exchange benefit.

It is usually the same as the **amount realized.** But if you have fixing-up expenses, these expenses are subtracted from the **amount realized** to determine the **adjusted sales price.**

EXAMPLE:

You sell your **old house** for $90,000, and have selling expenses of $6,000, and fixing-up expenses of $1,500. Compute your **adjusted sales price** so that you know how much the **replacement cost** of your **new house** must be in order for you to qualify for a tax-free exchange. . . .

Sales price	$90,000
Deduct selling expenses	6,000
Amount realized	$84,000
Subtract fixing-up expenses	1,500
Adjusted sales price	$82,500

This is the amount that your **replacement cost** must equal or exceed in order for you to qualify. In this example, your **replacement cost** of the **new house** must be $82,500 or more for you to qualify. Many people believe it's the sales price that must be reinvested, but it's not—it's the **adjusted sales price**.

A WORD ABOUT FIXING-UP EXPENSES

Sometimes people fix-up their **old house** to make it easier to sell, by painting, cleaning, etc. If you incur these kinds of expenses to make your **old house** more saleable, and if they are:

1. for work performed during the 90-day period ending on the date on which the contract to sell was made (usually the date on which you accept the offer)

2. paid for during the time period starting with the first day of the 90-day period and ending 30 days after the actual sale is completed

3. not deductible anywhere else on your tax return

4. not counted as improvements

then these fixing-up expenses are subtracted from the *amount realized* on the sale to determine your *adjusted sales price.*

CAUTION: This adjustment is made only in cases where the gain is postponed. Fixing-up expenses *are not deductible* in determining the actual gain on the sale of your *old house.*

Some examples of fixing-up expenses are: cleaning up the yard, painting (inside and outside), cleaning the carpets, and other expenses that are not deductible or counted as improvements.

The rule for qualifying for a full tax-free exchange on the sale of your *old house* is so important, we should review it again:

> **RULE:** You qualify for this tax benefit by purchasing and occupying a *new house* sometime during the 3-year *replacement time period* and your *replacement cost* is equal to or more than the *adjusted sales price* of your *old house.*

WHEN THE REPLACEMENT COST IS LESS THAN THE ADJUSTED SALES PRICE

If the *replacement cost* is less than the *adjusted sales price,* you might still qualify for a tax-free exchange on *part of the gain.* Here is the rule:

> **RULE:** If the *replacement cost* is less than the *adjusted sales price,* only the difference is recognized as gain. The gain is never more, of course, than your total gain on the sale.

Let's look at the 3 different situations that can happen to you. Assume that you have sold your *old house* for a gain of $28,000, and your *adjusted sales price* was $84,000:

	Situation 1	Situation 2	Situation 3
Adjusted sales price	$ 84,000	$ 84,000	$ 84,000
Replacement cost	**90,000**	**75,000**	**50,000**
Difference	$ None*	$ 9,000	$ 34,000
Total gain	28,000	28,000	28,000
Gain recognized	None	9,000	28,000
Gain postponed	$ 28,000	$ 19,000	$ None

*If the cost of the *new house* is higher than the *adjusted sales price,* there is no "difference" because *all* gain is postponed.

Situation 1: your *replacement cost* of $90,000 is more than the *adjusted sales price* of the *old house*. Therefore, all of the $28,000 gain is nontaxable, and you have a complete tax-free exchange.

Situation 2: your *replacement cost* of $75,000 is $9,000 less than the *adjusted sales price*. Since this amount is less than the $28,000 gain, the smaller amount of $9,000 is recognized as gain, and $19,000 ($28,000 gain minus the $9,000 recognized) qualifies for the tax-free exchange.

Situation 3: your *replacement cost* of $50,000 is $34,000 less than the *adjusted sales price*. Since the total gain on the sale was only $28,000, the entire gain is recognized, and you do not qualify for any tax-free exchange benefits. This is the situation when you do not purchase any *new house*. Your *replacement cost* would be zero.

18

No matter what you do or don't do after you sell your *old house,* you will always fall into one of these 3 situations. There are no others.

WHAT HAPPENS TO THE POSTPONED GAIN?

The postponed gain is simply postponed, and many times is never recognized for income tax purposes. It is passed through to your *new house* and reduces its *adjusted basis.* For example, if your postponed gain was $19,000, and you paid $75,000 for a *new house,* the original cost of the *new house* of $75,000 is reduced (for tax purposes only) to $56,000 ($75,000 less the $19,000). The $56,000 is your new *adjusted basis.* This is the amount you are allowed to deduct (instead of the actual original cost of $75,000) when and if you ever sell the *new house.* That's when they get you on the tax—or do they?

The tax-free exchange benefit on the sale of your personal residence is not a one-time benefit; it is available to you again and again, *just as many times as you qualify!* So, if you sell the *new house*—now it's your *old house*—you can qualify for a tax-free exchange and postpone the gain again, no matter how large the gain is.

Later we will see how your once-in-a-lifetime "over 55" exclusion can exclude all these postponed gains up to $100,000.

VERY IMPORTANT POINT: When you sell your *old house,* you determine how much your gain on the sale actually is. Nothing you do later changes this gain; it is fixed. No matter what happens, your gain is always the difference between what you receive for the house (the *amount realized*) and your total cost at the time of the sale (the *adjusted basis*). Again, nothing you do after you sell the *old house* changes this gain.

What you can change is the amount of this gain that is taxable in the year of sale! And you do this by buying a *new house* or taking maximum advantage of your once-in-a-lifetime "over 55" $100,000 exclusion.

MORE TALK ABOUT IMPROVEMENTS

It is very important to keep a record of the cost of the improvements you make to your house. You can deduct all of these costs when you sell the *old house.*

Typical improvements include: landscaping and shrubs, sprinkler systems, fences and walls, additional rooms, new heaters, air conditioners, swimming pools, and patios.

Many people overlook a hidden tax benefit when it comes to improvements. Look back at Situation 2, where your *replacement cost* was $9,000 less than the *adjusted sales price,* so the $9,000 difference was recognized as gain. (The total gain was $28,000.) How could you change this? The *adjusted sales price* was fixed; you got all you could for the house. But what about *replacement cost?* If that had been just $9,000 higher you would not have recognized any of the gain; all the gain would have been postponed. But the cost of the *new house* was only $75,000.

Let's see now, isn't the *replacement cost* the total of the original cost and the cost of all improvements added and paid for during the *replacement time period?* Right, and there it is—the cost of all improvements during this period, up to $9,000, will reduce the recognized gain, dollar for dollar. That's because it increases the *replacement cost* and therefore, reduces the "difference." And remember, it's the *difference* that is recognized as gain. In this Situation, get the *replacement cost* up $9,000 to a total of $84,000 (same as the *adjusted sales price* of the *old house*) and you would have a complete tax-free exchange on the sale, and the entire gain of $28,000 would be postponed.

To illustrate how this works, let's sell your *old house* and buy a *new house* just like in Situation 2. Then we will take 3 examples:

EXAMPLE 1: You add no improvements to your *new house* during the *replacement time period*

EXAMPLE 2: You add improvements costing $5,000

EXAMPLE 3: You add improvements costing $10,000

Let's see how much gain you must report on your tax return for each of
these 3 examples:

	Example 1	Example 2	Example 3
Adjusted sales price	$ 84,000	$ 84,000	$ 84,000
Subtract replacement cost:			
Original cost	75,000	75,000	75,000
Improvements	**None**	**5,000**	**10,000**
Total	$ 75,000	$ 80,000	$ 85,000
Difference (gain)	$ 9,000	$ 4,000	$ None

Notice that in Example 2, the $5,000 cost of improvements that you added
to your *new house* reduced the gain that you recognized on your *old house*
by $5,000. That's because you increased the *replacement cost* of the
new house.

The same is true for Example 3. The $10,000 worth of improvements
increased the *replacement cost* to more than the $84,000 required to receive
a full tax-free exchange.

That's how improvements added at the right time to your *new house* can
reduce the gain recognized in the year of sale on the *old house.* But don't
forget, you have to get the improvements in and paid for during your *replacement time period* in order to qualify.

TWO TAX TRAPS IN THE REPLACEMENT TIME PERIOD

There are 2 tax traps you should know about if you buy and/or sell more
than one *new house* during your *replacement time period:*

Tax trap 1: the last-of-more-than-one-replacement-residence rule

Watch out, a lot of people fall into this trap.

If you sell your *old house* at a gain, and buy more than 1 *new house* during the *replacement time period,* only the last one counts as your *replacement residence.* The house or houses in between will not count as a *replacement residence.* If you buy a *new house* and then sell it *before you sell your old house,* the *new house* will never qualify as your *replacement residence.*

EXAMPLE:

> Old house—sold July 1, 1979
>
> New house $\overset{\#1}{}$ —purchased and occupied July 15, 1979
>
> New house $\overset{\#2}{}$ —purchased and occupied August 1, 1980
>
> On July 15, 1979, when you purchased and occupied *new house #1,* it qualified as a *replacement residence* for the sale of your *old house.* However, because you purchased and occupied a second *new house* (#2) before the expiration of the 18-month time period, the second *new house* counts as the *replacement residence* and disqualifies *new house #1.* That means that *new house #1* is not your *replacement residence* anymore.

Look what this can do to someone who falls into this trap:

> *A homeowner sells her house for an adjusted sales price of $90,000. The gain was $40,000. She buys a replacement residence (let's call it R-1) right away for $110,000. Because R-1 cost more than $90,000, she qualifies for a tax-free exchange.*

*So far, so good! But suppose she goes out and buys another **new house** (R-2) and moves into it within 18 months from the time she sold **her old house**. The trap is sprung! R-2 becomes her **replacement residence** and cancels R-1. R-2 cost, let's say, only $68,000 (a difference of $22,000). Because R-2 becomes her **replacement residence** (instead of R-1), the difference of $22,000 ($90,000 **adjusted sales price** less R-2 cost of $68,000) will be recognized gain. In other words, R-2 cancels the tax-free exchange our homeowner had from R-1. And now she gets hit for lots of taxes!*

Remember the rule: If you buy and occupy more than one. **new house** during the **replacement time period,** only the *last one* will count as your **replacement residence.**

This can work the other way around, too. Reverse the costs of *R-1* and *R-2.* Now *R-2* qualifies our homeowner for a tax-free exchange on the sale of her **old house.** That's because *R-2* cost $110,000—more than enough to qualify. *R-1* cost only $68,000—not enough to qualify, but it was disqualified as her **replacement residence** anyway when she bought *R-2.*

Knowing ahead of time how tax benefits work can certainly be helpful, can't it!

Now, what happens if a homeowner sells *more than one* personal residence in an 18-month time period?

Tax trap 2: the single benefit rule

For most people, only one Section 1034 benefit is allowed in each 18-month period. If you sell your **old house** at a gain, and benefit from Section 1034, you cannot qualify for the same benefit on another sale if the sale is made within 18 months from the date of sale of the **old house.**

This example will help you understand:

> *You sell your **old house** at a gain, and the purchase price of your **new house** qualifies you for Section 1034 tax-free exchange benefits. If you sell your **new house** within 18 months after the date you sold your **old house**, the gain on the sale of the **new house** does not qualify for Section 1034 tax-free benefits. It's taxable.*

The Revenue Act of 1978 made a very important change in this single-benefit rule. Currently under this rule, if you sell more than one residence within 18 months, you can qualify for tax-free treatment *if the sale was made as part of a job-related move.* More on this later.

WHAT IF YOUR PROPERTY IS ONLY PARTIALLY A RESIDENCE?

If your property is used both for your personal residence and as income property, and you sell it, the transaction is treated as the sale of *2 properties:*

1. The personal residence portion qualifies for all of the benefits discussed here for personal residences.

2. The gain or loss on the income property portion is almost always recognized in full at the time of sale. It does not qualify for personal residence benefits.

Here is an example:

> *You own a 4-unit apartment building and live in 1*
> *unit. The other 3 units are rented to tenants. You*
> *sell the building; 25 percent of the transaction is the*
> *sale of your **old house**, while the other 75 percent is*
> *the sale of income property and subject to income*
> *property rules.*

BENEFIT FOR THE SELLER OVER 55

The Revenue Act of 1978 added a new major tax benefit for homeowners, called the "over 55" exclusion. Under the old law, there was a limited exclusion available to homeowners who were 65 years old or older when they sold their personal residence. This "over 65" exclusion was repealed. The effective date of these changes was July 27, 1978.

Under the current law, when you sell your **old house,** you can elect to exclude all or part of the gain, up to $100,000, if you meet two requirements:

1. Age requirement: you must be over 55 years of age *before* you sell the house. You can accept an offer on or before your 55th .birthday, but the sale *must* close *on or after* your birthday. (You are considered to be "over 55" *on* your 55th birthday.) If you are married, only one of you must be over 55. However, if both husband and wife are over 55, a double exclusion does *not* apply. You get only one.

    and

2. Use and ownership requirement: you must have owned and used the house as your principal residence for a period of time totaling at least 3 years within the 5-year period that ends on the date of sale.

In other words:

- Check the date you sold the house.

- Look back 5 years from that date.

- Did you own and live in the house at least 3 years during that 5-year period?

- If the answer is *no,* you do not qualify.

- If the answer is *yes,* you do qualify.

Remember, the exclusion is limited, and you get it only once. The excludable gain is limited to the *first* $100,000 of gain from the sale of your *old house.* And this is a once-in-a-lifetime election; you get to use it only *once.* And if you are married, only *1* exclusion is allowed, not 2.

Also, if you are married when you make the election, under the law, you have *both* used up your election. You can never make the election again, even if you are later married to someone else and your new spouse has never made the election. Nor can your new spouse qualify as long as you are married to each other, because as a couple, you are both considered to have made the election. The tax law treats a married couple as *1* taxpayer for purposes of this election. (That's why only 1 of you has to be 55 or over to qualify for the election.)

HOW TO SAVE GAINS
AND EXCLUDE THEM WHEN YOU ARE OVER 55

Here is another tax benefit that is overlooked by many people. Suppose you sell your *old house* when you are 45 years old, at a nice $40,000 gain. You surely don't qualify for the "over 55" exclusion, but you go right out and buy a *new house* and qualify for a Section 1034 exchange. It could look like this:

Purchase cost of new house	$125,000
Subtract postponed gain on sale of old house	40,000
Adjusted basis of new house for tax purposes	$ 85,000

Now let's say you live in your *new house* for 12 years and then sell:

Sales price	$190,000
Deduct selling expenses	15,000
Amount realized	$175,000
Deduct adjusted basis, as above	85,000
Gain on sale	$ 90,000

The actual gain on your *new house* was only $50,000 (It went up to $175,000 from the $125,000 cost), but your tax return will show the $90,000, because the $40,000 gain that you postponed when you were 45 years old now pops up. It certainly looks as if you are going to pay a lot of tax. But, on the day that the house was sold, you were over 55 years old, so you qualify for the once-in-a-lifetime election to exclude up to $100,000 of gain. This means that you can now exclude the entire $90,000 of gain *including the $40,000 gain you had 12 years ago* but postponed until now by buying a *new house!*

CAUTION: You are allowed to use this election only once. If you elect and exclude less than $100,000, you have used up your entire election. Say, for example, that you sell your *old house* for a gain of $60,000. You elect to exclude the gain under the "over 55" exclusion. It will cost you the entire $100,000 election to do it—it's all or nothing!

You really have to do a lot of thinking before you use your election. This is where the services of a well-qualified real estate professional can help you do the right thing at the right time.

A QUICK LOOK AT THOSE NICE CAPITAL GAINS

Let's stop and see how capital gains work. When you sell your *old house* at a gain, it's a capital gain. And if you had owned the house for more than 1 year before the sale date, you get a long-term capital gain.

Long-term capital gains receive very favorable treatment on your tax return. Let's say that you had no other capital gain or loss transaction last year and you sold your *old house* for a long-term capital gain of $60,000. You decide not to buy a *new house* and you are too young to use the $100,000 exclusion benefit. A wonderful thing happens to your gain of $60,000 on its way to taxable income—60 percent of it is non-taxable. That's right, 60 percent of your gain is excluded. It's called the net long-term capital gain deduction. The other 40 percent converts to ordinary income and adds to your taxable income.

Let's follow our example and see how it works:

Total long-term capital gain	$60,000
Subtract net long-term capital gain deduction (60 percent of $60,000)	36,000
Balance to taxable income	$24,000

And there's more good news. Under the Revenue Act of 1978, capital gains on the sale of your house are no longer subject to the minimum tax.

A WINNING COMBINATION

Sometimes you can take advantage of both the "over 55" exclusion and the tax-free exchange benefits at the same time on the same sale.

Let's say that after you sell the *old house* for an *adjusted sales price* of $180,000, you decide to buy another house, smaller and for less money, perhaps a condo or townhouse. Assume the *replacement cost* is only $70,000— a difference of $110,000 (*adjusted sales price* of $180,000 less the *replacement cost* of $70,000). So it looks like you have a recognized gain of $110,000. But remember the "over 55" exclusion—it's available if you want to use it!

Here's how it looks:

First the sale:	
Sales price	$195,000
Deduct sales expenses	15,000
Amount realized	$180,000
Deduct adjusted basis	40,000
Gain	$140,000

Then the 1034 exchange:

Adjusted sales price of old house - you had no fixing-up expenses	$180,000
Subtract replacement cost of new house	70,000
Difference	$110,000

Under Section 1034 rules, the difference of $110,000 is recognized gain; the other $30,000 ($140,000 gain less the $110,000 recognized) is postponed. However, the Revenue Act of 1978 permits you to elect to exclude gain on the sale up to $100,000. Let's apply this to the gain not postponed under your Section 1034 tax-free exchange benefit (the $110,000).

Now the combination:

Total realized gain	$140,000
Because you bought a new house, postponed gain	30,000
Gain not postponed	$110,000
"Over 55" exclusion	100,000
Balance—recognized gain	$ 10,000

This $10,000 is a long-term capital gain, and only 40 percent of it is taxable. That's only $4,000—not bad on a sale with a $140,000 gain! Who says the personal residence isn't a great tax shelter!

"REACHING BACK" FOR A TAX REFUND

Tax benefits can work in strange and mysterious ways. Here's one that lets you reach into the past, take back a gain on which you have already paid tax, and then exclude the same gain later under the "over 55" exclusion.

Here is what you must have to make it work:

1. You had already sold your *old house* before July 27, 1978.

2. You decided *not* to buy a *new house*, and therefore all your gain was recognized for tax purposes.

Here is what you can do to get your tax dollars back and pick up the gain later—tax-free:

1. Buy and occupy a *new house* sometime within 18 months from the date you sold your *old house*.

2. Make sure that the *replacement cost* is more than the *adjusted sales price* of your *old house*.

3. File a claim for refund of all federal income taxes paid on your original sale. (Happiness is a tax refund.)

4. Live in your *new house* at least 3 years.

5. Now, if you want to, you can sell the *new house* (assuming that you are over 55 years old) and qualify for your once-in-a-lifetime election to exclude up to $100,000 of gain. And that exclusion includes the gain you saved from that first sale, the one where you got your tax money back.

31

Let's look at an example and see how this works:

> *Let's say that you sold your **old house** on November 12, 1977, and recognized a gain of $48,000. This gain on your tax return cost you additional federal taxes of $11,700. One day, while talking to your real estate professional, you learn about the "over 55" benefit and how it works. You decide to buy a **new house** for $115,000 before May 12, 1979, so you can qualify for a Section 1034 tax-free exchange. Next, you file for a refund of the $11,700 taxes that you paid. The $48,000 gain is postponed into the **new house**. The cost **(adjusted basis)** of the new house is reduced by the $48,000.*
>
> *Now it's 1983, and you want to sell your **new house**. If you are over 55, you qualify to elect to exclude up to $100,000 of your gain, including the $48,000 you postponed back in 1977. That means that you can cash out, and put the money in your pocket (up to $100,000 of gain) tax-free. Looking at it another way, you save $11,700 in taxes by owning and living in the **new house** for just 36 months. That's $325 per month after taxes.*

Talk about tax shelters—this one is really hard to beat!

HOW TO DEDUCT SELLING EXPENSES AS A MOVING EXPENSE

Let's talk about expenses incurred in moving to a new place of employment. Wait a minute—what's this got to do with saving tax dollars when you sell your house? Plenty!

First, remember our discussion of the double benefit rule? If you sold more than 1 house in the same 18-month time period, only the *first house* qualified for the tax-free exchange, but not the others. The Revenue Act of 1978 changed all that; now the other sales will qualify for the benefit too, *if the sale is made as part of a job-related move.* What that means is that you must qualify for the moving expense deduction in order to take advantage of this double rollover benefit.

Also, if you qualify, you can deduct up to $3,000 worth of those *selling expenses* that we learned about earlier, right off the top of your regular income. And many times it's really easy to qualify. Here's a quick look at how to do it. (For a more detailed and complete coverage of this very important area of deductions, see your taxperson or call the IRS. They will be glad to help you.)

If you move in connection with your job or business, you qualify for moving expense deductions. These deductions include:

1. Direct costs: all reasonable direct costs of moving you, your family, and all your furniture. These direct expenses include all costs of moving your household goods and personal effects, and all moving costs paid to a moving company, including packing. If you move yourself, it includes only what you pay other people, like truck rental, etc. Your own labor is not deductible.

    Direct expenses include travel expenses for you and your family to the new job site area.

2. Indirect costs: subject to certain limitations you can deduct:

    a.) *selling expenses* on your *old house*

    b.) househunting trips to the new location area

c.) temporary living expenses in the new location area

You qualify for these moving expense deductions by meeting the following
2 requirements:

1. Your new job site must be at least 35 miles farther from your
    old house than was the old job site.

    For instance, your *old house* was 14 miles from your old job. To
    qualify, your new job must be at least 49 miles from your *old
    house* (35 miles plus 14 miles).

2. You must be employed in your new job for at least 39 weeks
    during the 12-month period following your move to the new area.
    Self-employment counts too, but there are some special rules.

There is no limit on the *direct cost* deductions as long as they are reasonable.

Your deduction for all *indirect costs* is limited to $3,000. This deduction
can include *selling expenses* of your *old house*.

Here is an example that shows how valuable this deduction can be for you:

> *This year you have taxable income of $25,000 plus a
> gain of $40,000 on the sale of your **old house**. Your
> **selling expenses** were $5,200. You qualify for the
> moving expense deduction.*

Now a comparison of how your taxable income would look depending on
how you deduct the *selling expenses:*

You buy a new house and qualify for a Section 1034 tax-free exchange:		
	Moving expense deduction	
	Yes	**No**
Taxable income	$25,000	$25,000
Moving expense deduction	3,000	None
Recognized gain on sale of old house	None	None
Taxable income	$22,000	$25,000

Notice that if you don't take the $3,000 as a moving expense, you just lose it this year and overpay your tax. And chances are that you will never get the deduction, even in future years.

You do not buy a new house:		
	Moving expense deduction	
	Yes	**No**
Taxable income	$25,000	$25,000
Moving expense deduction	3,000	None
Recognized gain on sale of old house	17,200(a)	16,000(b)
Taxable income	$39,200	$41,000

(a) Add back $3,000 *selling expenses* (deducted as a moving expense instead) to the $40,000 long-term capital gain—40 percent taxable of $43,000 is $17,200.

(b) 40 percent taxable of $40,000 long-term capital gain is $16,000.

REVIEW

Let's review together what we have just learned:

1. *Selling expenses* of your *old house* can be deducted directly from your regular income if you qualify.

2. The choice is yours—as a moving expense *or* as a reduction of the gain on the sale of your *old house. But you can't deduct it in both places—only 1!*

3. If you qualify for a Section 1034 tax-free exchange, you will waste the deduction if you *don't* take it as a moving expense.

4. If you don't buy a *new house* you will waste 60 percent of the deduction if you don't take it as a moving expense. Remember, 60 percent of your long-term capital gain is tax-free anyway. Why use the deduction here when it's 100-percent deductible as a moving expense?

A FINAL WORD

Income tax laws affecting the selling of your house is not an easy subject to understand. We all know that these laws and regulations are a big, complicated mess. Trying to comprehend them is like trying to grab a handful of fog—you know it's there, you can see it, but you can't get a grip on it no matter how hard you try.

In this book, I have explained as clearly as possible how these tax benefits can work for you when you sell your house. This knowledge can save you many of your hard-earned tax dollars. After all, that's what this book is all about—helping you save your tax dollars when you sell your house.

WORKSHEET 1—COMPUTING THE ADJUSTED BASIS OF YOUR OLD HOUSE

1. Enter the original cost of your old house—
   be sure to include closing costs incurred
   when you purchased the house. $ _____

2. Now enter the cost of all improvements
   you added to the property. $ _____

3. Total lines 1 and 2. $ _____

4. When you bought this house, did you
   postpone any gain on the house you
   sold before? If you did, record it here. $ _____

5. Did you ever deduct depreciation on the
   house—for example, as rental property
   or use as home office? If you did, record
   it here. $ _____

6. Did you ever deduct a casualty loss to
   your old house? If you did, record the
   total taken here. $ _____

7. Total lines 4, 5, and 6. $ _____

8. Now subtract the total in line 7 from
   line 3. The difference is your adjusted
   basis. $ _____

NOTE: Always fill out worksheets with pencil, so that you can erase when
you want to update the figures. The adjusted basis is a very important
figure—this is your cost deduction when you sell the property, and it
determines your gain.

Notes

WORKSHEET 2—COMPUTING THE GAIN ON SALE

1. Enter the sales price—the total con-   Date sold _____
   sideration you are receiving for the
   property. This price includes cash,
   notes assumed, and notes taken back. $ _____

2. Now enter the total selling expenses,
   which include sales commissions,
   recording fees, title policy fees,
   escrow fees, and all other expenses
   of this nature directly related to the
   sale of the old house. Do not include
   interest or real estate taxes paid;
   these are itemized deductions. Do
   not include personal items like in-
   surance or impound account money. $ _____

3. Subtract line 2 from line 1. This
   figure is the amount realized. $ _____

4. Now enter the adjusted basis from
   Worksheet 1—Item 8. $ _____

5. The difference is $ _____

This is your gain or loss on the sale of your old house. If the amount realized
is more than the adjusted basis, the difference is a gain; if the amount realized
is less than your adjusted basis, you have suffered a loss on the sale. And a
loss on the sale of your personal residence is not deductible. But today,
almost all sales result in a gain. It is necessary for effective tax planning that
you know how much gain you are realizing.

A word about the date sold that you recorded above—The replacement time
period starts 18 months before that date and ends 18 months after that
date. If you build your own replacement residence, you qualify for a 6-
month extension at the end of that period.

Notes

WORKSHEET 3—COMPUTING THE ADJUSTED SALES PRICE AND THE POSTPONED GAIN

1. Enter the amount realized
   (Worksheet 2—Item 3). $ _____

2. Enter the total of any fixing-up
   expenses you had that qualify. $ _____

3. Deduct line 2 from line 1. This is
   your adjusted sales price. $ _____

4. Write here the purchase cost of
   your new house. $ _____

   Is the cost of your new house more
   than the adjusted sales price?
   YES_____ NO_____
   If the answer is *yes,* stop here.
   You have a tax-free exchange, and
   the entire gain (see Worksheet 2)
   is postponed. If *no,* continue below.

5. Enter the amount by which your
   adjusted sales price (line 3) exceeds
   the cost of your new house (line 4). $ _____

6. Now enter the amount of your gain
   on the sale (Worksheet 2—Item 8). $ _____

7. The amount of gain not postponed
   and recognized this year for income
   tax purposes is the smaller of amounts
   at 5 and 6 above. Enter it here. $ _____

Remember, it's the total replacement cost that counts, not just the purchase cost of the new house. The amount at Item 7 above is the amount by which you might want to increase the replacement cost during the original replacement time period. You can do this by adding improvements.

Notes

Here is a handy schedule for recording improvements and their cost. Be sure to save all receipts and cancelled checks. You can count only what you pay others; your own labor does not qualify. Some people take pictures of the property before and after the improvement is added. Fences, walls, landscaping, trees and shrubs, added rooms, paneling, new heater, carpets, new roof, swimming pools, sprinkler system, air conditioner, paving—are all examples of improvements.

Kind of improvement	Date acquired	Cost or other basis

Notes

ABOUT THE AUTHOR

Richard A. Robinson received his B.S. degree in finance from Syracuse University and has been a practicing CPA in California since 1957. He has presented tax programs before thousands of real estate professionals, including the California, Arizona, and Wisconsin Associations of Realtors®, and the California, Nevada, and Nebraska chapters of the Farm and Land Institute. He has taught Income Tax Factors of Real Estate Investments for the UCLA Real Estate Certificate Program and is the author of several books about taxes and real estate.

Robinson has taught over 10,000 homeowners how to save tax dollars when they sell their house. His unique approach to the field, presented in a simple and enjoyable manner, has gained him national recognition both as author and teacher.